Jabber

Other Plays by Marcus Youssef

*Adrift**

The Adventures of Ali & Ali and the aXes of Evil: A Divertimento for Warlords (with Guillermo Verdecchia and Camyar Chai)*

Ali & Ali: The Deportation Hearings (with Camyar Chai and Guillermo Verdecchia)*

A Line in the Sand (with Guillermo Verdecchia)*

Chloe's Choice

Come Back to the 7-Eleven, Judy Blume, Judy Blume

How Has My Love Affected You?

King Arthur and His Knights (with Niall McNeil)

Leftovers (with Charles Demers)

Peter Panties (with Niall McNeil)

Winners and Losers (with James Long)*

* Published by Talonbooks

JABBER

a play by

MARCUS YOUSSEF

TALONBOOKS

Talonbooks
278 East First Avenue, Vancouver, British Columbia, Canada V5T 1A6
www.talonbooks.com

First printing: 2015

Typeset in Adobe Caslon
Printed and bound in Canada on 100% post-consumer recycled paper

Interior and cover design by Typesmith
Cover graphic by Antoine Yared, courtesy of Geordie Productions

Talonbooks acknowledges the financial support of the Canada Council for the Arts, the Government of Canada through the Canada Book Fund, and the Province of British Columbia through the British Columbia Arts Council and the Book Publishing Tax Credit.

Rights to produce *Jabber*, in whole or in part, in any medium by any group, amateur or professional, are retained by the author. Interested persons are requested to contact the author's agent: Colin Rivers, Vice-President, Marquis Entertainment, 73 Richmond Street West, Suite 312, Toronto, Ontario M5H 4E8, tel.: 416-960-9123, email: crivers@marquisent.ca

LIBRARY AND ARCHIVES CANADA CATALOGUING IN PUBLICATION

Youssef, Marcus, author
    Jabber / Marcus Youssef ; introduction by Dennis Foon.

A play.
Issued in print and electronic formats.
ISBN 978-0-88922-950-1 (PAPERBACK). – ISBN 978-0-88922-951-8 (EPUB)

    I. Foon, Dennis, 1951–, writer of introduction II. Title.

PS8597.O89J33 2015   C812'.54   C2015-904161-9
                                                          C2015-904162-7

For Amanda F.

FOREWORD

More than one million Muslims live in Canada and the vast majority are peace-loving people, moderate both in religion and politics. Yet they are tarred with the same brush as a tiny minority of Islamic extremists whose actions, thousands of miles away, dominate Western headlines. It has a troubling effect: a recent Angus Reid poll showed that nearly half of Canadians continue to hold an unfavourable view of Muslims – and that negative sentiment is rising. This is a sentiment that transforms fellow law-abiding citizens into the "other," vulnerable to suspicion, discrimination, and violence, as witnessed on September 17, 2013, when three teenagers violently assaulted a seventeen-year-old girl in St. Catharines, Ontario. The provocation: the victim was wearing a hijab.

Such is the troubling context of Marcus Youssef's important, heartfelt, smart, and funny play. At its most elemental, the well-observed *Jabber* is an opportunity for the audience to break down their preconceptions about Muslim faith and community through the experience of Fatima, a Muslim girl. Even the title is a means to deconstruct the mystery of the hijab, for the girls who wear them have created their own slang word for the scarves – jabbers. Fatima, the young woman at the centre of the story, is never untrue to the meaning and power of the hijab in her life. This cloth that covers the hair is a sign of respect, of humility to God. But like so many kids caught between cultures, Fatima both honours and resents her differences. At one point, she tells the audience: "Sometimes, all I want is to be just like everyone else."

Both Fatima and her boyfriend, Jorah, live under a cloud. For her it's because of her religion; for him, because of his past. With humour and wit, Youssef deftly shows how the two outsiders are pulled together – and apart – because of their otherness. Both are being smothered by assumptions and preconceptions. It's assumed that Fatima's parents will physically harm her if they discover her relationship with Jorah, that she's a victim, a suppressed female. While in Jorah's case, since his father is in jail for physically abusing his wife, people conclude that Jorah was also assaulted and has inherited his father's proclivity towards violence. So both are considered time bombs, viewed with wariness and concern. This weighs on the two and impacts their everyday lives. The better we get to know them, the more unfair this burden feels.

Though her relationship with Jorah is in some ways an act of rebellion, Fatima's actual commitment to the hijab is unwavering, she wears it as an emblem of who she is and where she came from. Her removal of it to show Jorah her hair is an act of profound intimacy. In an age when naked selfies are ubiquitous, her action is both poignant and ironic. To the unschooled Western eye, it's inconsequential; but by this point in the story we know Fatima well enough to realize the significance of what she does – and the depth of Jorah's betrayal – when he posts a picture of her uncovered head on the Web.

One of the wonders of *Jabber* is its gentle touch. It's a drama grappling with an incendiary topic but the entire piece exudes compassion. Fatima and Jorah make mistakes but the consequences aren't cataclysmic – they're realistic. He hurts her, they break up, he apologizes, the door is left open a crack for their future. When Jorah finally explodes, he hits a locker, not a teacher. Fatima – and we – fear her parents will punish her horribly for having been exposed on the Web without her hijab. From what we've seen in the media, we might even fear she'll be murdered for dishonouring them. But this is a stereotype, no more indicative of the nature of people who identify as Muslim than Jorah's father's violence is indicative of the nature of Judeo-Christian identified Canadians. An assumption that leads many to fear all that is Muslim, justifying the suppression of human rights, including mass surveillance, renditions, and torture. In Fatima's case, her parents are justifiably disturbed, but her punishment is totally sensible and appropriate, in line with what any responsible parent might do. The tension comes from our expectation of irrational violence – and that is exactly Youssef's point. We've been conditioned to expect the worst. The sensitivity in the storytelling exposes the lie.

At its heart, *Jabber* is a love story. Fatima and Jorah echo Romeo and Juliet. And like Shakespeare's classic, this play examines how social forces can tear young love apart. At a time when tension is high and misunderstanding rife, *Jabber* arrives, gently pointing at one way of addressing the horrific gap between the Islamic and Western worlds: by looking into each other's eyes.

— DENNIS FOON
Founding director, Green Thumb Theatre

Jabber was commissioned by Geordie Productions under the artistic direction of Dean Fleming. It was developed with the dramaturgical support of Playwrights Workshop Montreal and the financial support of the Cole Foundation. Originally produced by Geordie Productions, *Jabber* first toured high schools and colleges across Quebec and Eastern Canada from September 2012 until April 2013, with the following cast and crew:

FATIMA	Mariana Tayler
JORAH/MELISSA's FRIEND	Ian Geldart
MR. EVANS	
HISTORY TEACHER }	David Sklar
MELISSA	

Directed by Amanda Kellock
Dramaturgy by Emma Tibaldo
Set and costumes designed by James Lavoie
Lights designed by Ana Cappelluto
Sound designed by Amanda Kellock

Geordie's production of *Jabber* subsequently toured to Young People's Theatre in Toronto in November 2013, and was presented as a spotlight performance at the International Performing Arts for Youth (IPAY) showcase in Pittsburgh, PA, in January 2014. It then toured Maine and Vermont in November 2014. At that time Aris Tyros replaced Ian Geldart as Jorah.

Manitoba Theatre for Young People produced *Jabber* on the main stage October 15 to 23, 2014, and on tour October 27 to December 19, 2014, with the following cast and crew:

FATIMA	Adele Noronha
JORAH/MELISSA's FRIEND	Kristian Jordan
MR. EVANS	
HISTORY TEACHER }	Cory Wojcik
MELISSA	

Directed by Ann Hodges
Set, costumes, and props designed by Sean McMullen
Lighting and video designed by Hugh Conacher
Music composed by Joseph Aragon
Stage managed by JoAnna Black

Green Thumb Theatre produced the play on tour in Vancouver and across British Columbia in the fall of 2015, directed by Patrick MacDonald.

CHARACTERS

FATIMA, a teen girl

JORAH, a teen boy

MR. EVANS (Mr. E), the school counsellor

MELISSA, a student at the new high school

MELISSA's FRIEND, another student at the new high school

HISTORY TEACHER

All teenagers are about sixteen years old.

Melissa and her friend should be played by the actors playing Jorah and Mr. E.

In addition to these roles, at times the three actors also comment on the action, noted in the text as Actor One, Actor Two, and Actor Three. The actor who plays Jorah plays One, Fatima plays Two, and Evans plays Three.

The actor playing Mr. E. also plays the History Teacher.

A high school, Jorah's place, Fatima's place, the "duct."

Generally, the text and Facebook messages have been projected, as if the characters are sending them live. This has worked well. Geographic name references should be changed to reflect the location(s) of each production. At some point, cultural references might need to be updated as well. Contact the author for further information or suggestions.

JABBER

SCENE 1
LET'S SAY

ACTOR ONE, ACTOR TWO, and ACTOR THREE speak to the audience.

ACTOR ONE
Hey. I'm (*actor name*).

ACTOR TWO
Hey. I'm (*actor name*).

ACTOR THREE
I'm (*actor name*).

ACTOR TWO
Let's say we're in a high school.

ACTOR ONE
Oh look, we are.[1]

ACTOR TWO
Let's say I'm not twenty-four years old.[2] But sixteen.

ACTOR THREE
And I'm not twenty-seven. But thirty-four.[3]

ACTOR TWO
Old.

ACTOR ONE
Let's say her name is Fatima.

---

1   When performing in a theatre, cut this line.
2   Change to reflect actor's actual age.
3   Ditto.

ACTOR TWO
Let's say when kids hear that, sometimes they ask –

ACTOR ONE
Fatima, huh? Is it okay if I call you Fat?

ACTOR THREE
Let's say she's learned to laugh. And say –

FATIMA
Sure, no problem. Is it okay if I call you a-hole?

ACTOR ONE
Let's say when we say "a-hole." you know what we mean.

ACTOR TWO
Let's say Fatima's only been in Canada for a couple of years.

ACTOR ONE
Let's say the country she's from is, like, nine thousand
kilometres away –

ACTOR TWO
And there was some kind of war –

ACTOR THREE
Or revolution –

ACTOR ONE
Or whatever –

ACTOR THREE
Let's say her parents just forced her to switch schools and
come to this one because of something that happened at
her old school –

ACTOR ONE
Something bad.

FATIMA
Not bad, just stupid. I was walking with my friends. Seema
and Hama and Lindsay. Lindsay's a white girl, but she
hangs out with us. We call ourselves the jabbers. Cuz of the
hijab. Ha ha.

So we're walking, and ignoring people on the street who
look at us – they always do. When we get to school, there's a
bunch of teachers standing around and, like, four police cars
and a pile of cops. Standing around the wall outside the gym.
Staring and pointing and talking into their walkie-talkies.

They sent us home. For our "own safety." My parents
totally freaked out. They were, like, "You are not safe, you must
change schools." I was, like, "What are you talking about?
It was just some graffiti." "No! It was a threat, Fatima. You
must remember: these people are full of hate."

I told them, "Hama and Seema's parents aren't making
them change schools. And there's no jabbers at St. Mary's, not
even one." My mom's, like, "What is this, a jabber? Three years
in Canada and you don't sound like our daughter, you sound
like one of these stupid girls we see in the mall."

I said, "A jabber is what we what we call the dumb thing
you make us wear on our heads." Bad idea. My father went
crazy, goes, "You are disrespecting God." (*to God*) Sorry.
(*to audience*) I'm lucky my father didn't kill me. He said,
"You are my daughter. I will do whatever necessary to
protect you from these animals."

By forcing me to come here, a subway and two buses from
where we live. St. Mary's. Where's there's no Seema, or Hama.
No jabbers at all.

Let's say today is my first day.

ACTOR ONE
Let's say my name is Jorah.

ACTOR TWO
    Let's say Jorah's in grade 10.

ACTOR THREE
    Let's say he's that guy that people are a little afraid of –

ACTOR TWO
    Rumours –

ACTOR ONE
    He did something –

ACTOR THREE
    Or something happened to him –

ACTOR TWO
    Something bad.

ACTOR THREE
    Let's say maybe none of those rumours are true –

ACTOR TWO
    Or maybe they are.

ACTOR ONE
    Let's say today he got in trouble –

ACTOR THREE
    Again.

ACTOR TWO
    He was in history class –

ACTOR ONE
    They were studying the Holocaust –

ACTOR TWO

And the teacher was telling them about what happened to Jewish people in World War Two, how the German army put them in gas ovens.

ACTOR THREE

Jorah wasn't paying attention.

ACTOR ONE

He was looking out the window, at a kid playing on the soccer field with a little ball.

ACTOR TWO

And the teacher noticed Jorah not listening, and that pissed him off, because Jorah never listens. So he called him out, in front of everybody –

HISTORY TEACHER
  What do you think of that, Jorah?

JORAH
  Huh?

HISTORY TEACHER
  The Nazis taking people – real, living human beings –
  and baking them alive in ovens.

JORAH
  You mean, like pizza?

HISTORY TEACHER
  I beg your pardon?

JORAH
  Little mini dudes, all covered in cheese.

HISTORY TEACHER
  Do you even know what you're saying?

ACTOR ONE
  It was one of those things that came out of Jorah's mouth.

ACTOR THREE
  Not because he hates Jewish people –

ACTOR TWO
  But more like –

ACTOR ONE
  Whatever.

ACTOR THREE

And because he hates how teachers always look at him,
like he's already done something wrong.

ACTOR ONE

Let's say Fatima was in the class –

ACTOR THREE

And on their way out, Jorah noticed her looking at him.

ACTOR TWO

And he stared at her, for a while.

ACTOR ONE

Because of her scarf.

JORAH stares at FATIMA.

FATIMA

I know what they're thinking. You know how you can catch
somebody's eye, just for a second, and you can see exactly
what's in their head? Same as you, probably. "Whoa. What's
with the scarf? I bet she has to wear it. I wonder if she's a
terrorist. I bet she's really, like, timid and any of those things."
(*to JORAH, challenging*) Hi.

JORAH

Yo.

FATIMA

(*to audience*) I'm not shy. But it's also, hijab, it's part
of who I am.

ACTOR ONE

Let's say we're actors.

ACTOR TWO

Let's say there's three of us –

ACTOR ONE

And about two hundred of you.[4]

ACTOR THREE

Let's say I'm a guidance counsellor. Let's say my name is Evans, but kids call me Mr. E. Let's say I like my job, and most kids pretty much like me.

At some point FATIMA comes to speak to EVANS.

EVANS
Mr. Porteous.

JORAH
Mr. E.

EVANS
Aren't you're supposed to be waiting for me in my office?

JORAH
Is that a trick question?

EVANS
No.

JORAH·
Then yeah, I am.

EVANS
Mind telling me why you're not there?

JORAH
You're not going to like my answer.

EVANS
Really?

JORAH
You're going to think I'm, like, testing your authority.
But I'm not.

EVANS
Try me.

JORAH

Okay. I got this massive zit. On my butt. It's huge. And when I go to your office, your secretary lady – Mrs. Gaspo –

EVANS

Gasperini.

JORAH

That's worse, dude. She always makes me sit down while I wait.

FATIMA

Mr. Evans.

JORAH

If I sit on the zit, I swear, my butt's gonna explode.

EVANS

(*to FATIMA*) Excuse me.

JORAH

I'm not lying. I'll show you –

FATIMA

Uh, the principal told me to come see you.

JORAH starts to take off his pants.

EVANS

(*to JORAH*) Stop it! My office. Now! (*to FATIMA*) Fine, no problem. You too. I'll be right there.

JORAH enters. FATIMA waits.

JORAH
  Where's Evans?

FATIMA
  I don't know.

JORAH
  Of course.

  He sits.

FATIMA
  How's your butt?

JORAH
  Fine. Oh. (*gesturing to her scarf*) Are you allowed to say "butt"?

FATIMA
  I just did.

JORAH
  You're new.

FATIMA
  Yeah.

JORAH
  If you're planning on blowing up the school, I'm in.

FATIMA
  Excuse me?

JORAH
A lot of kids would thank you. You'd be a hero. You know what? I'll help. I'm ready. Just give me the signal. Nobody'll suspect me cuz I don't look like a terrorist.

FATIMA
Like me.

Beat.

JORAH
I'm just kidding around.

FATIMA
Ha ha.

JORAH
I shouldn't even joke about blowing up the school. They probably have microphones in here. Get myself locked down.

FATIMA
Yeah.

JORAH
What's your name?

FATIMA ignores him.

JORAH
Oh, I get it. You don't want to blow your cover.

FATIMA
Sorry?

JORAH
You'd be a crap terrorist if you told people your real name. It's cool.

FATIMA
Ha ha. Fatima.

JORAH
Fatima.

FATIMA
Yeah.

JORAH
Mind if I call you Fat?

FATIMA
No. Mind if I call you a-hole?

JORAH
That's funny.

FATIMA
Thank you. I get to say it a lot.

JORAH
"A-hole."

FATIMA
What?

JORAH
Nothing.

FATIMA
You think because I'm Muslim, I can't swear?

JORAH
A-hole's not exactly a swear. You got, like, some wicked forehead zits? Covering up some major pus bombs? That why you got the head thing?

FATIMA
My scarf?

JORAH
Yeah.

FATIMA
It's part of my religion.

JORAH
It's called a Taliban, right?

FATIMA
Taliban? Oh my God. Now that's funny.

JORAH
What?

FATIMA
Taliban are the guys who are fighting in Afghanistan.
It's called a hijab.

JORAH
Oh. Do you wear it all the time? I'm just asking.

FATIMA
Yes. Sort of.

JORAH
In the shower?

FATIMA
No.

JORAH
In bed?

FATIMA

I only have to wear it in public. I don't wear it at home.

JORAH

Is it to stop you from turning guys on?

FATIMA

Oh my God.

JORAH

Isn't that it?

FATIMA

It's to show humility. Before God.

JORAH

Is it, like, those Taliban guys might think you're so hot, they'd see your hair and just, like, lose control? I saw this old Chuck Norris movie where they catch a bad, like, Muslim Taliban dude and tie him up and force bacon down his throat. It was pretty funny.

FATIMA

Huh. I saw this movie once about this dumb white boy who talked about a lot of crap he wasn't smart enough to understand. Oh hang on, that wasn't a movie. That's what's happening right now.

EVANS enters.

EVANS

Sorry, I'm late. I trust Jorah is behaving.

FATIMA

Not really.

JORAH
    What? We're just getting to know each other.

EVANS
    Here's the form. I'm sorry, I haven't had time to give you
    a proper welcome. Let me assure you that you're safe at
    St. Mary's, and we're going to do everything we can to make
    your transition a smooth one. Right, Jorah?

JORAH
    For sure. What happened?

FATIMA
    Nothing. By the way, if you say any more weird, racist, or
    insulting things to me, I will use my terrorist skills to kick you
    in the crotch so hard you'll be down on your knees begging for
    your life. Just sayin'. (*exiting*) See ya.

        Beat.

EVANS
    She just called you racist.

JORAH
    I asked about her scarf.

EVANS
    Actions have consequences.

JORAH
    We were just joking around.

EVANS
    There's a pattern here.

JORAH
    What are you talking about?

EVANS
Murdering Jewish people in ovens is like making pizza.

JORAH
I was joking.

EVANS
Mr. Levy is Jewish. He had family members executed by the Nazis. So, shocking though this may be for you to hear, for Mr. Levy a joke about Jews being murdered in the Holocaust isn't actually all that funny.

JORAH
He was giving me attitude.

EVANS
Because you weren't paying attention.

JORAH
He's boring.

EVANS
I could suspend you. Ask your mother to come in.

  Beat.

EVANS
How is she, your mom?

JORAH
Fine.

EVANS
Really?

JORAH
Yeah. I'm sorry, okay? Is that what you want me to say?

EVANS

What I want isn't the point.

JORAH

Oh.

EVANS

Actions have consequences.

JORAH

So you keep saying.

EVANS

Look. I know what you've been through.

JORAH

No, you don't.

EVANS

It's your anger, Jorah. Like we've talked about. You need to be very careful. Because of who you are. And what people know. The girl with the headscarf – (*mispronouncing her name, but trying not to*) Fateema – you know why she transferred here?

JORAH

No.

EVANS

You should find out.

JORAH

That it?

EVANS

For now.

> *JORAH gets up to leave.*

[20]

JORAH
Worst thing I can imagine ... Being a teacher. By the way, her name is Fatima.

JORAH walks downstage, as if to do a monologue.

JORAH
(*to audience*) Blah blah blah blah blah.

ACTOR ONE, ACTOR TWO, and ACTOR THREE speak to the audience.

ACTOR THREE
Let's say Fatima felt a little confused after her run-in with Jorah.

ACTOR TWO
He was kind of a dick.

ACTOR ONE
But also kind of funny and smart.

ACTOR THREE
Let's say she went home, and her parents asked her about her first day.

FATIMA arrives home. Speaking to her parents, on her way to her room.

FATIMA
It was fine, thank you. I'm going to my room. Homework. I've got a ton!

FATIMA's in her room. She goes directly to her computer.

FATIMA
My parents think I talk like that to everybody. "You are always right, all I want to do is absolutely every little thing you ask."
    We moved to Canada three years ago. I was thirteen. You climb on a plane, fly for two days, and you land in the middle of winter. I'd never seen snow in my life. I spent a lot of time on my computer. Convinced them I needed it in my

room – for homework. They don't know how easy school is in Canada. It is.

(*looking at the computer*) There's a webcam on a building in our country. In Cairo, the city where we're from. The streets are packed. Twenty million people there. That's like five Torontos. In the distance, you can see the corner of the girls' school I went to before we left. I keep it open. Sometimes I see friends I had there, just walking down the street, holding their books, laughing and talking. I like it better here. Most of the time. My father wanted me to go to a girls' school here, but we couldn't afford it. Thank God. He drives a taxi. In our country he was an engineer.

I spend a lot of time in my room. Looking at the webcam. And on Omegle. Or TeenChat.

I don't talk. I just watch. Teenagers, from all over the place, just hanging out. They're all white. That's how I learned to speak English. Watching them: girls, talking to guys that they know. And guys they don't. I watch them. Flirt and smile and make faces. "Oh my God, what? No! I love you. You can't tell them."

It's shocking, what these girls do. In their own houses, with their parents in another room.

(*turning back and then calling out*) I told you, homework! (*to audience*) They're not as smart as they think.

I watched this blonde girl. With a friend, talking to some guy. She took off her shirt. Sat there, in her bra, going, what do you think, do you like them, oh my God, they're so small! In her bra. And then … She took pictures. And texted them to the guy who watched. Is that normal? Not for jabbers …

She gets a Facebook message.

JORAH
look … sorry if i was dick. uh, is that ok to say to you? ha ha. friend me, but only if you want. maybe I'll see you around.

JORAH and FATIMA.

JORAH
Hey, Fat.

FATIMA
That's not my name.

JORAH
Joke. Evans called you "Fateema."

FATIMA
Right.

JORAH
You didn't friend me.

FATIMA
I was busy.

JORAH
Is that a different scarf?

FATIMA
I have more than one.

JORAH
Good thing. Otherwise it'd start to reek. But it's, uh, it's nice.

FATIMA
I have to go.

JORAH
Yo, I'm sorry if I pissed you off yesterday. I didn't mean anything. I was just joking around.

Beat.

JORAH
All right?

FATIMA
Sure.

JORAH
Evans said some big deal thing happened at your old school.

FATIMA
Maybe.

JORAH
That why you transferred here?

FATIMA
It was nothing.

JORAH
Must have been pretty bad to make you want to come to this dump.

FATIMA
I guess.

JORAH
What?

FATIMA
Graffiti. On the wall of the school.

JORAH
   That's it?

FATIMA
   It said, "All Muslims must die."

JORAH
   Whoa.

FATIMA
   Yeah. My parents went crazy.

JORAH
   Did it freak you out?

FATIMA
   I guess.

JORAH
   I'm not like that, eh? I mean I know I got a reputation and stuff, but I'm not into being against people and the racism stuff. I want you to know that.

FATIMA
   All right.

JORAH
   If it had said "All teachers must die" that would be different. I'd be good with that.

FATIMA
   Uh … okay.

JORAH
   Joke.

FATIMA
Funny.

JORAH
Thanks. You make any friends yet?

FATIMA
Sure. A couple.

JORAH
Liar. I've seen you.

FATIMA
It's the scarf. It weirds people out.

JORAH
Yeah.

FATIMA
You're basically the only one who's talked to me.

JORAH
What do you have next?

FATIMA
Uh, math. We both do.

JORAH
Gonna skip. Go down to the duct.

FATIMA
Oh yeah.

JORAH
It's the place the bad kids like me go.

FATIMA
That what you are – bad?

JORAH
That's what I hear. You want to come?

FATIMA
I shouldn't.

JORAH
It's a pretty cool spot. Nobody'll be there. There's a little river, sun shining through the trees. Kind of like a park. See, I'm not all bad.

FATIMA
I can't miss class.

JORAH
Okaaay … See ya round.

    Beat.

FATIMA
You always wear your hoodie like that?

JORAH
I don't know. I guess.

FATIMA
Makes you look like that guy in *South Park* … Kenny.

JORAH
Shut up.

FATIMA
It does.

JORAH
  That's a snowsuit. And who watches *South Park*?

FATIMA
  Me. Sometime you should try pulling it down.

JORAH
  Whatever.

FATIMA
  Then people could see your face.

  Maybe she goes to help him.

JORAH
  Okay, fine.

  He does, reluctantly.

FATIMA
  For a big a-hole, you're actually kind of cute.

  A moment. JORAH leaves. FATIMA speaks to the audience.

FATIMA
  In grade 7, my parents found a book of mine in my room. I'd written "I love Jeff Payette" all over it, a million different times. I didn't even know Jeff Payette. He was in grade 8 and every girl in my class had a crush on him. My parents said that if they ever caught me alone with a boy they'd lock me in my room and never let me out. Can you imagine? Sometimes, all I want is to be just like everyone else.

*ACTOR ONE, ACTOR TWO, and ACTOR
THREE speak to the audience. FATIMA is also there.*

ACTOR TWO
Let's say Jorah split and went down to the duct.

ACTOR THREE
And Fatima went to class, where Ms. Anderson, the math
teacher, asked her to get up in front of everybody and explain
why she wears a hijab.

FATIMA
I said, what? In front of everybody? I tried to be honest. I was,
like, it's part of who I am, and it also reminds me of where I
come from. She said, "Don't you think wearing it means that
men in your culture think they can control you." I said, "I don't
know, don't you think those disgusting sweaters you always
wear mean that people think you're a pathetic dork." Except
I didn't actually say that. I said, "I don't really see it that way.
But I understand your point."

ACTOR THREE
Let's say on her way out Fatima got ambushed by a couple of
grade 10 girls.

ACTOR ONE
Let's say when we put on these wigs, we're those girls.

ACTOR THREE
Let's say we know that's kinda weird.

They put on wigs.

MELISSA
Hey.

FATIMA
    Hi.

MELISSA
    We love your scarf.

MELISSA's FRIEND
    It's so pretty.

FATIMA
    Thanks.

MELISSA
    Quick question.

MELISSA's FRIEND
    At your old school –

MELISSA
    Did you really get attacked by skinheads?

FATIMA
    Uh, no.

MELISSA's FRIEND
    That's what we heard.

MELISSA
    They chased you down with metal pipes.

MELISSA's FRIEND
    Beat you over the head.

MELISSA
    You were in the hospital.

MELISSA's FRIEND
    And have massive brain damage.

MELISSA
Shut up. She's exaggerating.

FATIMA
It was just some graffiti.

MELISSA
That's good.

FATIMA
I guess.

MELISSA
Better than being hit with a pipe.

MELISSA's FRIEND
What did the graffiti say?

FATIMA
"All Muslims must die."

MELISSA's FRIEND
Eww. That's so racist.

FATIMA
Yeah.

MELISSA
Weird.

FATIMA
Anyway ...

MELISSA
We noticed you talking to Jorah.

MELISSA's FRIEND
A lot.

MELISSA
Do you like him?

FATIMA
Sure. I mean, I guess.

MELISSA
I'm Melissa.

FATIMA doesn't know what that's supposed to mean.

MELISSA
Don't tell him I talked to you, okay?

FATIMA
Why not?

MELISSA
He'll freak.

MELISSA's FRIEND
Yeah. He's an okay guy, but …

MELISSA
All the stuff that happened.

FATIMA
What?

MELISSA
He didn't tell you?

MELISSA's FRIEND
Of course not. It'd freak her out. He knows that.

MELISSA
Friendly advice: be careful. He's not always as nice as he seems.

FATIMA
  What do you mean?

MELISSA's FRIEND
  We gotta go.

FATIMA
  No, hang on. What are you talking about?

MELISSA
  See ya.

FATIMA
  Bye.

ACTOR THREE
  Let's say that night, Fatima was up in her room, like usual –

ACTOR ONE
  She told her parents she had a big history assignment, about
  the Holocaust –

ACTOR TWO
  Let's say that, despite what the girls told her, she decided to
  become Jorah's friend.

JORAH and FATIMA text or instant message each other.

JORAH
yo

FATIMA
hi kenny

JORAH
shitup.

JORAH
shutup i mn

FATIMA
ha =) whr u?

JORAH
home

FATIMA
me2 skype?

JORAH
k

They can now see each other and are speaking over Skype or some kind of video chat.

FATIMA
Ta da.

JORAH
Hey. Nice scarf.

FATIMA
Thanks. I tied it Jordanian style.

JORAH
What's that?

FATIMA
Duh. A country. Jordan. It's near where I'm from.

JORAH
Which is, like, what? Mongolia?

FATIMA
Oh my God. That is so ignorant. Mongolia is next to China. Do I look Chinese?

JORAH
No.

FATIMA
Exactly. I'm from Egypt.

JORAH
Oh. Like with pyramids and stuff. What?

FATIMA
It's not just pyramids. It's one of the world's oldest civilizations.

JORAH
Yeah, you ride camels.

FATIMA
Oh my God. We invented math. And paper. And condoms.

JORAH
Seriously?

FATIMA
I shouldn't have said that.

JORAH
It's cool. But you do ride camels. I've seen pictures.

FATIMA
Only tourists ride camels. They're nasty. They spit everywhere and try to throw you off. More people ride donkeys.

JORAH
Damn.

FATIMA
Yeah. But we had a car. If you have enough money, you get a car. Or motorcycles. With whole families riding on them, like, four or five people hanging on. And no traffic lights. Not really any laws at all. People just drive and honk. When we moved here, it was so embarrassing. My father would go crazy fast, honking at everybody, and speed through red lights. He got, like, three tickets in a week.

JORAH
Cool.

FATIMA
I guess. That your room?

JORAH
Yeah.

FATIMA
Your parents there?

JORAH
No. Yours?

FATIMA
Always.

JORAH
They're strict.

FATIMA
You have no idea.

JORAH
It's like some Muslim thing.

FATIMA
Yours just let you do what you want?

JORAH
Pretty much.

FATIMA
Lucky.

JORAH
I guess.

FATIMA
Some girl asked me about you today.

JORAH
Who?

FATIMA .
Wanted to know if I liked you.

JORAH
What did you say?

    Beat.

JORAH
Okay, I see.

FATIMA
I'm not even allowed to date guys.

    He laughs.

FATIMA
What?

JORAH
"Date." You sound like you're in grade 5.

FATIMA
Shut up. If my parents knew I was even talking to you, they'd
kill me. And they'd kill you too.

JORAH
They'd have to find me first.

FATIMA
They would. They'd track you down.

JORAH
Seriously?

FATIMA
Oh yeah. They'd go all ISIS on you.

JORAH
Ha ha. You could stand up to them. Tell them it's different
here. You have a right to do what you want.

FATIMA
It was Melissa who asked me about you. About us.

JORAH
Oh.

FATIMA
Did you go out?

JORAH
Not really. For a while.

FATIMA
She said something weird.

JORAH
No doubt.

FATIMA
That I should be careful.

JORAH
Of what?

FATIMA
You.

JORAH
I dumped her.

FATIMA
Why?

JORAH
Because she bored the crap out of me.

FATIMA
Uh … okay.

JORAH
So she's pissed. That's all. Besides, it's the sort of thing you'd only talk about to someone you really trust, you know. Like, if you were going out.

   Beat.

JORAH
But we're not.

FATIMA
That's true, we're not.

JORAH
Right.

FATIMA
   Yeah.

JORAH
   You're really pretty. And not just pretty. Smart too.

   Beat.

JORAH
   And I got to say: the whole Muslim thing? It's kind of
   super-hot.

FATIMA
   (*to audience*) He's really sweet. Right? And every girl in this
   dumb school, if they think some guy's sweet, they can just tell
   him and, if he likes her, then they hang out, and … But me?
   I'm at home hiding in my room pretending to do homework,
   doing every little thing I'm told.

ACTOR ONE
   Let's say Fatima and Jorah hung out at school a lot.

ACTOR TWO
   And Jorah would try to get her to come to the duct.

ACTOR THREE
   But she'd say, "I can't. I can't miss class. My parents
   would freak."

ACTOR TWO
   Until a couple of days later, when she changed her mind.

JORAH and FATIMA are together.

JORAH
Nice, eh? It's a river that runs under the whole city. They covered it up, except for this spot. Here you can see out, but nobody can see in. Evans followed me here once, but I hid up in there, and he never found me.

FATIMA
Wow.

JORAH
Relax, it's all good.

FATIMA
Yeah.

JORAH
It's just one class. Nobody cares. You know that, right?

FATIMA
Okay.

JORAH
Trust me. I know.

FATIMA
I bet you do.

JORAH
Shut up.

FATIMA
If we got marks for skipping, you'd be like a genius.

JORAH
I'm not stupid.

FATIMA
I'm just bugging you!

JORAH
Very funny.

FATIMA
Ha ha.

JORAH
That's where I live, right up there. (*gesturing towards his apartment*) My whole life. You look really good right now, in the sun, the shadows, they make you look … pretty.

FATIMA
Good line. But not really.

JORAH
I googled how to talk to Muslim girls. It said to tell you I saw your hair, so that means you have to marry me. Melissa's dumb friend, she walks right up to me, goes, "She's Muslim, you know." I'm, like, "Yeah." and she goes, "Yeah, dumbass. That means you'll never get any."

FATIMA
Gross.

JORAH
Is she right?

> *Beat.*

FATIMA
I guess it depends what you mean by "any."

JORAH
    I don't know.

FATIMA
    Me neither. It's weird how people act like they know
    something about Islam, when they don't have a clue.

JORAH
    I don't.

FATIMA
    I know.

JORAH
    I'd guess you're not supposed to be this close to a guy.

FATIMA
    You're smarter than you look.

        Something happens, they are touching?

JORAH
    Does this mean we're going out?

        Something that tells us yes.

EVANS and FATIMA are talking.

EVANS
Fatima. How are things going?

FATIMA
Uh, fine.

EVANS
You're adjusting all right?

FATIMA
Sure, yeah.

EVANS
I know you weren't too happy about coming to St. Mary's.

FATIMA
It's okay.

EVANS
You've skipped a couple of classes.

     Beat.

FATIMA
Are you going to tell my parents?

EVANS
I'm supposed to.

FATIMA
Please don't.

EVANS
What would they do?

FATIMA
Kill me.

EVANS
What do you mean by that? Would they – hurt you?

FATIMA
Huh?

EVANS
How harshly would you be punished?

FATIMA
I don't know.

EVANS
It's important. I need to know what you think they would do.

FATIMA
I've never skipped a class before in my life.

Beat.

EVANS
Can I ask you a personal question?

FATIMA
I guess.

EVANS
Are you and Jorah going out?

Beat.

EVANS

I know that when you're new to a school and when something traumatic has happened, like the graffiti incident, you can feel the pressure to fit in.

FATIMA

I'm fine.

EVANS

Jorah's not a bad person, don't get me wrong. But I'm not sure he's right for someone like you.

FATIMA

What do you mean "someone like me"?

EVANS

Do your parents know about your relationship?

FATIMA doesn't answer.

EVANS

I've known Jorah for a long time. He's been through a lot. It's not his fault, but ... I think you should be very careful. Really.

Beat.

EVANS

For now, just for a bit – why don't you try giving Jorah a little more space?

Beat.

EVANS

Will you think about it?

FATIMA

I have to go home.

EVANS
    Look – do yourself a favour. Ask Jorah about his dad.

FATIMA
    His dad?

EVANS
    Yes, his dad.

> *JORAH and FATIMA text or instant message
> each other.*

FATIMA
  hey

JORAH
  tay

FATIMA
  what

JORAH
  thinking
  @ u.

FATIMA
  me2

JORAH
  sup?

> *Now they videochat.*

FATIMA
  Hi.

JORAH
  Smile.

FATIMA
  What?

JORAH
  Just do it. Please?

> *She smiles.*

JORAH
  Nice.

FATIMA
  What?

JORAH
  Screenshot. You look awesome.

FATIMA
  Thanks.

      Beat. JORAH checks his phone.

FATIMA
  Thanks for being ... cool.

JORAH
  Always.

FATIMA
  You know what I mean.

JORAH
  Not really.

FATIMA
  Patient. With me. You know.

JORAH
  You're welcome.

FATIMA
  I've never done this before.

JORAH
  No!

FATIMA
Shut up! Back home I wouldn't have even thought about it.
There would have been no way. But here ... it's like everyone
can do whatever they want.

JORAH
You're not like anybody I've ever known. That's ... it's what I
like about you.

FATIMA
It's what I like about you too. Hey, so, the weirdest thing
happened today.

JORAH
What?

FATIMA
Something I overheard ... somebody was talking
about your dad.

JORAH
What did they say?

FATIMA
Nothing I could understand, just ...

JORAH
What? Was it Melissa?

FATIMA
No.

JORAH
Who?

FATIMA
Some other kids.

JORAH
Just standing there talking about my frigging dad?

FATIMA
Kind of.

JORAH
What?

FATIMA
Don't be mad. I just – overheard them.

JORAH
Saying what?

FATIMA
I couldn't understand it.

JORAH
Who was it?

FATIMA
I told you –

JORAH
What did they look like? Were they in our grade?

FATIMA
Why does it matter?

JORAH
Melissa.

FATIMA
No, Jorah, it wasn't.

JORAH
Who else?

     Beat.

JORAH

People think they know. They think they know about him, and
me. But they don't. They don't know anything.

Beat.

FATIMA

You can trust me.

Beat.

FATIMA

I've never – what we're doing – this? If my parents found out,
I'd be dead. For me to do – even this – with a boy, it's the most
shameful thing they could imagine. And I know you don't
understand, but if I'm going to do that, I need to know who
I'm doing it with.

JORAH

You're not like your parents, right?

FATIMA

Yeah.

JORAH

Totally different.

FATIMA

Yeah, I mean, in a lot of things.

JORAH

Me too. I'm different than my dad too.

FATIMA

Tell me.

Beat.

JORAH
    He's inside.

FATIMA
    Inside what?

JORAH
    Duh. Jail. That freak you out?

FATIMA
    No.

JORAH
    Liar.

FATIMA
    What did he do?

JORAH
    Stuff.

        A long beat.

JORAH
    I was in grade 7. I was in my room, and they were fighting
    in the kitchen, and I was on the computer, and so I put my
    headphones on. Didn't hear it. Except one thing, at the end.
    A smash. I looked down the hall. Mom was holding her face,
    and there was broken stuff on the floor, and he was pacing
    back and forth. He was crying, and throwing shit, and yelling
    he was sorry. All at the same time.
        I ran outside. Went to the duct. It's where I always went.
        At school, I had to go to all these counsellors. They'd
    always ask me questions, like, "How do you feel." I'd be, like,
    "I don't know."
        After, people looked at me different. I'd catch a teacher
    staring at me. Kids too. Like I was dangerous. Like they had
    a reason to be scared. I changed schools but people hear, they

find out. It was all over the news. If you google our name, it's what comes up.

He got three years, with no parole, because they said it wasn't the first time. That there was a "pattern of abuse." Which I guess is true. But honestly, until I heard the ambulance that day, I hadn't ever really noticed. Just sat in my room, with my headphones on, not really thinking about much at all.

FATIMA
Oh Jorah.

JORAH
What?

FATIMA
I don't know. I'm so sorry.

JORAH
Shit happens.

FATIMA
I guess. Did he ever … hurt you?

JORAH
No. I mean, I don't know. Not really.

FATIMA
I don't know what to say.

JORAH
Nobody does.

FATIMA
That must be so hard.

JORAH
Whatever. I guess.

FATIMA
Jorah.

Beat.

FATIMA
I won't tell anyone.

Beat.

FATIMA
Trust me.

She texts.

JORAH
Okay.

FATIMA blows a quick kiss.

FATIMA
I trust you.

JORAH
I trust you too.

FATIMA
I know what it's like to have people think you're a freak.

FATIMA blows another kiss.

FATIMA
To want to be like everybody else.

She starts to remove her hijab.

FATIMA
I trust you. Oh my God.

She shows more of her hair.

JORAH
Fatima –

FATIMA
I trust you.

> *FATIMA is now showing all her hair. She makes the sign of a heart.*

> *Music.*

> *FATIMA is alone onstage.*

ACTOR THREE
Let's say that night Fatima had a dream.

> *In the dream, they start to make out, tentatively at first, then passionately. JORAH pushes further. She tries to signal enough, or to stop him. He keeps pushing. Music builds. It is big, epic.*

FATIMA
Stop!

JORAH and FATIMA text or instant message each other.

JORAH
yo

FATIMA doesn't respond.

JORAH
u n calc?

FATIMA doesn't respond.

JORAH
wn2 chill

FATIMA doesn't respond.

JORAH
wru

FATIMA
;)

JORAH
;) ?

MELISSA approaches FATIMA.

MELISSA
Jorah's looking for you.

FATIMA
Oh, thanks.

MELISSA
How are things going?

FATIMA
Fine.

MELISSA
You sure? He's having trouble finding you.

FATIMA
No, everything's good.

MELISSA
I'm glad. I'm not jealous, you know. You guys are such a cute couple. I really want you two to work.

JORAH and FATIMA meet.

JORAH
Hey.

FATIMA
Hi.

JORAH
I've been trying to find you.

FATIMA
Yeah, sorry, I just ...

JORAH
I brought you something.

FATIMA
Oh?

JORAH
A surprise.

FATIMA
Cool.

JORAH
That was all right, last night.

FATIMA
Yeah.

JORAH
What?

FATIMA
Nothing.

JORAH
You have really pretty hair. Joke. Here. (*handing her a print of a photograph*) It's the screenshot.

JORAH moves in for a kiss that FATIMA rejects.

JORAH
What?

FATIMA
You can't show this to anybody.

JORAH
I'm not. I'm giving it to you.

FATIMA
I could get in so much trouble.

JORAH
You trust me, remember?

FATIMA
You don't understand.

JORAH
What?

Beat.

FATIMA
Last night, after, I had this dream, that we were … making out.

JORAH
Sounds fun.

FATIMA
It wasn't. I kept telling you to stop, but you wouldn't.

JORAH
It was a dream.

FATIMA
I shouldn't have taken off my scarf.

JORAH
Why not? I didn't ask you to.

FATIMA
I know.

JORAH
You did it. You wanted to. You want to.

FATIMA
I know!

Beat.

JORAH
What's the big deal?

FATIMA
My whole life, that's what.

JORAH
Your whole life?

FATIMA
And my family, and my religion. What I did is a sin –

JORAH
You're talking like we slept together –

FATIMA
A sin against God.

JORAH
Showing me your hair?

FATIMA
You don't understand. For someone like you, it's impossible.

JORAH
Someone like me?

FATIMA
Yes.

JORAH
An a-hole with a criminal dad.

FATIMA
That's not what I meant –

JORAH
Right.

FATIMA
You don't understand –

JORAH
All I do is try to understand.

FATIMA
I couldn't sleep, I was up all night and, I know that's weird, but all the girls you go out with, like Melissa –

JORAH
Melissa?

FATIMA
We're too different.

    Beat.

JORAH

I guess Melissa was right.

FATIMA

What do you mean?

JORAH

About me not getting any. Weird thing is, for the first time in my life I didn't even try. (*showing her the photograph*) "The most beautiful girl in the world." That's what I wrote on it. (*ripping up the photograph*) There. Now you're safe.

FATIMA

I'm sorry.

JORAH

One thing. I want to know – which kid was talking shit about my dad?

Beat.

JORAH

You owe me.

FATIMA

It wasn't a kid. (*to audience*) Last summer we went back to Egypt to see our family for the first time. I'd forgotten what it was like to walk around the streets and not have people stare at me like I'm a freak. I was normal again, just like everyone else. That felt really weird.

This is a climactic scene. It should feel heightened, symphonic, and kind of mythic – the moment past and present come together. You might consider breaking the convention and having ACTOR ONE, ACTOR TWO, and ACTOR THREE act out some of the almost-violence as they narrate it, somewhat blurring the distinction between character and storyteller.

ACTOR THREE

Let's say when Jorah started thinking –

ACTOR TWO

About how Mr. E has no right to tell people about his family, and what's gone on with him –

ACTOR ONE

No f-ing right at all.

ACTOR THREE

And let's say when Jorah started thinking that, he couldn't stop, because of the injustice of it, and a feeling in his gut, and the voice in his head that kept talking about it, over and over again.

ACTOR TWO

Let's say he spent most of the afternoon planning his ambush –

ACTOR ONE

Let's say it was almost the end of school.

ACTOR THREE

Let's say Jorah was waiting outside Mr. E's office, where they've got the really hard chairs.

FATIMA
What are you doing?

JORAH
Nothing, I just want to talk to him.

FATIMA
You can't.

JORAH
Really? Cuz this is a free country. But maybe you don't
realize that.

FATIMA
It doesn't have anything to do with your dad.

EVANS
Jorah. Is everything okay?

JORAH
Awesome.

ACTOR TWO
Let's say Jorah started talking to Mr. E –

ACTOR THREE
And pretty soon he was yelling.

ACTOR ONE
Let's say Mr. E tried to calm him down, and pretty soon there
was a bit of a crowd gathered around.

ACTOR TWO
Let's say Jorah made threats so somebody called the
principal –

ACTOR ONE
Because they'd all heard stories about what happens when an
angry kid goes psycho in a school –

ACTOR ONE
And let's say that Jorah cocked his fist –

ACTOR THREE
And Mr. E put up his hands –

ACTOR TWO
And let's say he was just about to pound the crap out
of Mr. E –

ACTOR THREE
When he got a flash, or a picture, in his head –

ACTOR TWO
About what used to happen –

ACTOR ONE
A while ago –

ACTOR THREE
At his home –

ACTOR TWO
When he was hiding in a corner, not wanting to look, but not
being able to help it –

ACTOR THREE
Watching his dad beat the crap out of his mom.

ACTOR ONE
Let's say Jorah didn't hit Mr. E –

ACTOR TWO
But punched the metal locker instead –

ACTOR THREE
Hard enough to dent it –

ACTOR ONE
And hurt his hand pretty bad.

ACTOR THREE
Let's say the principal was the first one to get there –

ACTOR TWO
The gym teacher was behind him, trying to catch up –

ACTOR THREE
Because the gym teacher was kind of out of shape.

ACTOR TWO
They were both running up the hall, calling his name,
and yelling –

ACTOR THREE
In that way adults do –

ACTOR TWO
When they think things are about to get bad.

ACTOR THREE
Let's say Jorah yelled back –

ACTOR ONE
"A-hole" –

ACTOR THREE
And a few other things too –

ACTOR ONE
That are a little more real.

ACTOR TWO
He took off in the other direction –

ACTOR THREE
With the gym teacher and principal in hot pursuit –

ACTOR TWO
And Fatima, in the hall, watching them go …

ACTOR THREE speaks to the audience as JORAH texts on his phone.

ACTOR THREE
Let's say Jorah ran straight to the duct, because that's where he always goes.

FATIMA arrives. JORAH's still texting on his phone.

FATIMA
Hey. That gym teacher didn't stand a chance. Too fat.
Your hand –

JORAH
Don't you have to get home?

FATIMA
Yeah.

JORAH
See ya.

FATIMA
Who are you texting?

Beat.

JORAH
My dad. He gets out this week. He keeps texting me. "I want to see you. You're my son."

Beat.

FATIMA
Whoa.

JORAH
What do you think I should do?

FATIMA
I don't know.

JORAH
I thought you knew everything.

FATIMA
No.

JORAH
We had these counsellors. They were always, like, your father
is a violent man. You're going to want to forgive him, but
you can't. That will just encourage him. It'll make it more
likely that he'll do it again. But people aren't always what you
think they are.

FATIMA
You should talk to somebody.

JORAH
But not you.

FATIMA
Yeah. For sure. I mean, as friends.

JORAH
Because I got mad? Because I punched a locker? Because my
dad's an a-hole? Because you showed me your hair?

FATIMA
No, it's not about you. Can't you see? It's because of me.
It's about me.

An awkward moment.

FATIMA
Talk later?

JORAH doesn't respond.

SCENE 17
THE NEXT THING JORAH DID

ACTOR ONE, ACTOR TWO, and ACTOR THREE speak to the audience.

ACTOR THREE
Let's say the next thing Jorah did he felt like he was doing it because of love.

ACTOR ONE
Let's say that night Fatima got a text from Melissa.

ACTOR THREE
It said –

ACTOR TWO
Check Facebook. Now!!!!!

ACTOR THREE
Let's say Fatima followed the link.

ACTOR TWO
It was a new page.

ACTOR ONE
"My Muslim ex-girlfriend takes off her hijab."

ACTOR THREE
Let's say Jorah had recorded their chats.

ACTOR TWO
Not really for any reason –

ACTOR ONE
More like just because it felt like a secret –

[72]

ACTOR TWO
And because sometimes he hates how girls treat him –

ACTOR THREE
Like he's already done something wrong.

ACTOR ONE
Under the video was a caption –

ACTOR THREE
It said, "Actions have consequences."

ACTOR TWO
Let's say the page spread fast –

ACTOR ONE
And let's say Fatima told Mr. E, and he got Facebook to
shut it down.

ACTOR THREE
Let's say Mr. E called Fatima's parents. Let's say Fatima's
parents freaked out, and Mr. E talked to them for a long time.

ACTOR TWO
Let's say as he was talking to them, Mr. E was thinking
about a Muslim family in another part of the country who
murdered their two daughters because they thought they had
dishonoured their family by being sluts.

ACTOR ONE
Let's say there's almost two billion Muslim people in
the world.

ACTOR THREE
Let's say they're not all the same.

FATIMA

I showed my parents. It was the hardest thing I've ever done. I said, "All I did was blow kisses and show him some hair." I was crying, but I was, like, "What's the big deal? Is that really so bad? Do you know what girls do online." They said, "No, we don't." Of course not. I was, like, "Well, you should look sometime." Next day they told me my punishment. No more computer in my room.

ACTOR THREE

Let's say Fatima's parents surprised her.

ACTOR TWO

Let's say some kids might have downloaded the video, but it didn't go viral.

ACTOR ONE

Let's say Fatima's parents let her go back to her old school and reunite with Seema and Hama and Lindsay.

ACTOR TWO

Let's say when people talked about the video, they exaggerated, and rumours spread that made it sound way more explicit than it was.

ACTOR THREE

Let's say Fatima decided to ignore them and focus on her friends, and after a while the rumours kind of went away.

ACTOR TWO

Let's say sometimes people do bad things that they regret.

ACTOR THREE

Let's say a couple months later Jorah texted Fatima.

JORAH

I'm sorry.

ACTOR TWO
Let's say Fatima took two days to answer.

FATIMA
Oh?

JORAH
Stupidest think I've ever done. I was mad. I'm
soooooooooooooo sorry.

ACTOR THREE
Let's say there's something about the way he texted,
like, twenty-five Os so that made her agree to meet him,
at the duct.

JORAH and FATIMA meet.

JORAH
  You get in trouble?

FATIMA
  Yeah.

JORAH
  I'm so sorry.

FATIMA
  You said that.

JORAH
  Are you okay?

FATIMA
  Good to be back with the jabbers. You?

JORAH
  I saw my dad.

FATIMA
  Really?

JORAH
  First time in three years. I never visited him when he
  was inside.

    Beat.

JORAH
He said he was really sorry. He told me sometimes people do things they wish they could take back. Then he asked me to talk to my mom. Ask her if she'd see him. So they could talk.

FATIMA
Did you?

JORAH
No. Sometimes it takes more than sorry.

FATIMA
Yes.

JORAH
See you around?

FATIMA
Don't know.

JORAH
As friends?

FATIMA
Maybe.

JORAH
Thing is, I have seen your hair. So we have to get married.

FATIMA
That's a joke, right?

JORAH
Yeah.

FATIMA
Very funny.

JORAH
   Ha ha.

ACTOR THREE
   Let's say they may have gotten together again after that.

ACTOR TWO
   Or maybe not.

ACTOR ONE
   And let's say –

ACTOR THREE
   The end.

   Music rises.

ACKNOWLEDGEMENTS

Special thanks: Dean Fleming, Emma Tibaldo, and Amanda Kellock, for their invaluable contributions to the development of this play. Barry Cole, Amanda Fritzlan, Sumayya Kassamali, Guillermo Verdecchia, and Zak and Oscar Youssef.

DENNIS FOON

Dennis Foon is a Detroit-born playwright, novelist, producer, and screenwriter. He was the founder and artistic director, from 1974 to 1986, of Vancouver's Green Thumb Theatre, a company that soon evolved into a cutting-edge theatre with an award-winning repertory of plays about the reality of young people and the dilemmas they face.

Marcus Youssef's dozen plays and performance events have been produced in theatres and festivals across North America, Europe, and Australia, from New York to Dublin to Berlin. His awards include Rio-Tinto Alcan Performing Arts, Chalmer's Canadian Play, Arts Club Silver Commission, Seattle Times Footlight, Vancouver Critics' Choice Innovation (three times), as well as numerous local awards and nominations for best new play, production, and director in Vancouver, Toronto, and Montreal. Marcus has been artistic director of Vancouver's Neworld Theatre since 2005, where he also co-founded Progress Lab 1422, a collaboratively managed, six-thousand-square-foot studio and production hub. Youssef has served as an assistant professor at Montreal's Concordia University and implemented Canada's first join Bachelor of Performing Arts degree program at Capilano University. He was the inaugural chair of Vancouver's Arts and Culture Policy Council, teaches regularly at the National Theatre School of Canada and Langara College's Studio 58, and is an editorial advisor to *Canadian Theatre Review*. Youssef lives in East Vancouver with his partner, teacher Amanda Fritzlan, and their sons Oscar and Zak.